"I LOVE HIM, BUT..."

"He growls at the dog, just to make it clear who's the boss."

—ELEANOR, NEW HAVEN, CT

"I LOVE HIM, BUT..."

BY MERRY BLOCH JONES

WORKMAN PUBLISHING · NEW YORK

Library of Congress Cataloging-in-Publication Data

I love him, but…— / [collected] by Merry Bloch Jones.
p. cm.—ISBN 0-7611-0102-0
1. Men—Quotations, maxims, etc.
2. Husbands—Quotations, maxims, etc. I. Jones, Merry Bloch.
PN6084.M415   1995   305.31—dc20   95.34379   CIP

*Workman books are available at special discounts
when purchased in bulk for premiums and sales
promotions as well as for fund-raising or
educational use. Special editions or book excerpts can
also be created to specification. For details,
contact the Special Sales Director at the address below.*

Workman Publishing Company, Inc.
708 Broadway, New York, NY 10003-9555

Manufactured in the United States of America
First Printing September 1995

10 9 8 7 6 5 4 3 2 1

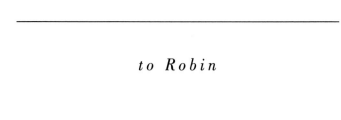

to Robin

ACKNOWLEDGMENTS

This book could not have been written without the inspiration of Mona Rosenfeld and Heddy Kahn, the enthusiasm of Connie Clausen and her staff, the expertise of Sally Kovalchick and Lynn Brunelle, and the candor of the married people who eagerly revealed pieces of their private lives.

I also received encouragement from Lanie Zera, Ruth Waldfogel Farbach, Karen Greenfield, Susan Stone, Sue Small, Nancy Delman, Jane Braun, my mom (Judy Bloch), my sister (Janet Martin), and the three who make my world turn—Robin, Baille, and Neely.

Finally I want to thank my late father, Herman S. Bloch, and my late brother, Aaron N. Bloch, who, as the first men I loved, prepared me well for the "buts."

WIVES' TALES

Three of us had been cackling, once again, at the expense of our husbands.

"It can't be just us," Heddy decided. "Look around. Look at the men most women are married to. Are you going to tell me those guys don't make their wives nuts?"

Mona thought about it. "Yeah. I guess, when you put it that way, it could be a whole lot worse."

We sighed, smirked, consoled each other and speculated about whether every "happily married" woman endured similar spousal gripes. "It can't be just us," we insisted. "Can it?"

And so, in the interests of science and sanity, I undertook to find out. Before the day was over, I'd delicately asked a dozen women whether their husbands annoyed them in any way. Without hesitation or reflection, a dozen women spilled forth long lists of aggravating qualities and habits with which they'd been struggling since the honeymoon. By the end of a week, word had spread. Women throughout the area were calling me to enumerate their husbands' most irritating quirks.

More research followed. I called friends in New England, California, Florida, Washington, D.C., Chicago and New York. They contributed their lists, often along with those of their friends, acquaintances and relatives. I asked for input by E-mail; women across the country responded with gusto. Women spoke up at the beauty parlor, the school, the playground, the pool. At parties, in waiting rooms, at the mall, in ladies' rooms. On trains, in planes. Interviews happened spontaneously, anytime, anyplace, anywhere I came face to face with married women.

Sometimes, husbands were present and joined in, happily reminding their wives of their most maddening habits or irritating quirks. One helpful man broke in, in mid-sentence: "Hey—how about the way I always interrupt you—"

In all, over two hundred married women, coast to coast, participated. They are mothers, grandmothers, stepmothers and women without children. They've been wed for at least six years and range in age from twenty-seven to seventy-six. Middle- and upper-middle-class, some are full-time homemakers; others have careers outside the home. They vary in race, religion, income, educational background and geographic location. Despite their differences, however, all share enthusiasm for unloading their pent-up marital peeves.

When asked what annoys them about their husbands, most women smile. Often their eyes gleam and hands twist as they answer. Some actually salivate. One grabbed my arm, as if to steady me so I wouldn't swoon or try to escape when I heard her reply. In general, answers poured forth with relish and abandon, candor and hilarity, and a definite playful, conspiratorial tone.

Most spouse-loving, successfully married wives freely admit that their husbands, at least some of the time, make them absolutely, nail-bitingly, hair-pullingly nuts. They describe wedded bliss as paradoxical balance between affection and affliction, desire and disgust, friendship and frenzy.

This balance is nothing new. As brides, most of us enter our marriages starry eyed and hopeful, our vision obscured by romantic notions. Sometime after the honeymoon, however, reality begins to set in. To our shock and dismay, we find holes in our beloved's socks and rust on his armor. We discover, in short, that Prince Charming has flaws.

The comments that follow form a tapestry of wifely inspiration, insults and insights. It is my hope that this clear, unadulterated picture of Mr. and Mrs. America will tell us something about who we really are, and pay tribute to the powerful marital bonds to which more than half of us remained committed.

"He follows me around the house like a lost puppy. If I turn around, I bump into him. If I stop too quickly, he bumps into me."

—IRIS, PITTSBURGH, PA

CLOSE QUARTERS...

WITHIN FOUR WALLS

The road into the sunset, for many women, is lined with junk and electronic toys. Their husbands will not throw out anything, from old magazines to torn socks, broken appliances to rusty screwdrivers. Some discover that, privately, Mr. Right eats with his mouth open, cracks his knuckles, bounces his knees, jingles his coins, bites his nails, picks at his toenails, or paces.

Most women complain that cohabitation leads to inevitable conflicts of dominance, control, territory and power. Competition arises in various forms; personal time, space and identities become difficult to define. With experience, however, most successful wives gain skills at balancing intimacy with individuality, retaining both closeness and closet space, and caring for both the outer man and his inner child.

"He's a kid, a big kid. He has every gadget there is. He's a salesman's dream. He's got three big screen, high-resolution TVs, and a couple of tiny ones the size of cigarette packs. The house is full of cellular phones, some still in the boxes, a few that never worked. CD players. Snowblowers. Electric lint removers. Blood pressure cuffs. Gum ball machines. A juke box. Electric juice squeezers. Bread bakers. Half a dozen contraptions for cleaning your teeth and gums—he's big on that. Video cameras of every size. And I haven't even gotten to the computer stuff yet."

—KATE, BETHESDA, MD

"Whenever he walks in the door, he turns on everything. The TVs, the CDs, the radio, the lights in every room. The place blazes. If I turn a TV off because no one's watching it, his mouth will drop in amazement and he'll ask, 'Why'd you do that?' "

—TILLY, BROOKLYN, NY

66**H**e comes in and leaves a trail of stuff through the house. Shoes, jacket, tie, briefcase, mail. Strewn wherever."

—MAVIS, ALLENTOWN, PA

"He saves things. He loved our cat. So he saved her hairballs. Cat's been dead ten years. He's still got her hairballs in his night-stand."

—CLAUDIA, VALLEY STREAM, NY

"My husband can't part with anything. His nightstand's stuffed with magazines dating from three and four years ago. The closet's bursting with his old clothes. He has a fit if I throw out anything or give it away, but he has shirts that have yellowed with age, the fabric frayed away to nothing. Torn pants that don't even fit him. Socks where the elastic's crumbled and gone. He doesn't wear this stuff, it's just there. Disco shirts. Bell-bottoms. Leather pants. He could open a museum."

—MARTHA, MADISON, WI

"He has every tool ever made or sold in this century down in the basement—cartons, shelves, drawers full. Half of them are rusted, I'm sure. They've never been used. He just can't resist a hardware store. Our basement should be given to the Smithsonian."

—CAROL, SKOKIE, IL

"He freaks out if there's clutter. He had wall-to-wall closets filled with shelves built in our family room so we could stack things in there and close the door. He insists that the house look like a magazine picture. But I can't ever find anything. It's all stuffed into a closet somewhere."

—MILDRED, ELIZABETH, NJ

66 **W**hen something breaks, he saves it 'for parts,' just in case. Our cellar is a graveyard for broken appliances. Computers, coffee makers, televisions, radios, a refrigerator, washing machine. When I die, he'll probably keep me down there, too, in case he needs 'the parts.' "

—SYLVIA, EVANSTON, IL

"I LOVE HIM, BUT..."

"He can't resist a 'bargain.' When he had back surgery, he couldn't do anything but watch TV for a few weeks. We're still getting packages from the Home Shopping Network."

—DENA, PHILADELPHIA, PA

"He loves his clothes. Takes better care of them than of me. His shoes are all on trees, and each pair's covered. He polishes new shoes before he wears them. His suits are aligned by fabric and color. His handkerchiefs, ties—everything's in perfect order. If one shirt is hung in the wrong spot, if one handkerchief is misfolded, he gets nervous, goes nuts."

—SUSAN, BROOKLYN, NY

"I LOVE HIM, BUT..."

66 He tapes everything off the television, but he never labels the tapes. If you want to find a movie, you've got to play thirty tapes until you chance upon the one you want."

—DEIRDRE, GLADWYNE, PA

"His stuff expands to fill the available space. There's never a cleared counter. Mail, bills, receipts, phone numbers, business cards, manila folders, magazines, catalogs, brochures cover every square inch, from the entranceway through the kitchen to the bathroom and the bedroom. If I stack it up or move it, I 'lose' important papers. I prepare dinner on top of layers of paperwork. So that's tomato paste, not blood, on our phone bill."

—LORRAINE, CHEVY CHASE, MD

"I LOVE HIM, BUT..."

"**H**e's like a little boy playing with toy cars, only his cars are bigger and they cost a lot more. He gets all the magazines. Studies the auto section of the paper. In the nine years we've been married, he's had three motorcycles, a jeep, four mini-vans, two sports cars, two convertibles, a pickup truck and an RV. He has to have fancy wheels."

—ELLEN, INDIANAPOLIS, IN

"When I get into his car, I never know what I'll sit in. There's half-eaten snacks and garbage everywhere and the ashtrays stink. I don't want to put a foot inside because my shoes will stick to the floor."

—SISSY, MILWAUKEE, WI

"He drinks his coffee in the car every morning. I can't find any cups for my coffee, because he never brings them back. If you look in his car, you'll see two dozen cups, all growing things."

—MADDIE, TULSA, OK

"**H**e never cleans his car. It's full of trash. Candy wrappers, lollipop sticks, soda bottles. On Father's Day I had it washed and waxed. I vacuumed the rug and polished the dashboard. He didn't even notice."

—AMELIA, WAUKEGAN, IL

"If there's been a frost at night, he warms the car up for half an hour. Then he gets in and revs the engine."

—MARILYN, BOSTON, MA

"I LOVE HIM, BUT...."

66 **W**hen he gets a cold, he takes to his bed. Wraps himself up and pouts, sulks like a helpless baby, waiting for 'Mommy' to make him all better."

—JANE, ST. LOUIS, MO

66 **W**hen I'm sick with the flu, vomiting all day, he comes home and says, 'Aw. I guess this means no dinner, huh?' "

—CALLIE, DES MOINES, IA

"No matter how ill he is, he won't take an aspirin. He's afraid it'll 'mask' his symptoms. Which he lists, in great detail, as they develop."

—TAMMY, BALTIMORE, MD

66 He's a walking pharmacy. Daily, he takes about forty different holistic health products. He lectures me about bee pollen and avocadoes. Edible flowers. Roots, the healing powers of garlic. He carries vials of pills with him wherever he goes and pops vitamins into his mouth all day long. And he says, 'A capsule a day,' about six times an hour."

—LESLIE, SEATTLE, WA

"I LOVE HIM, BUT..."

"When he eats, he won't let any one food on his plate touch another. If it does, he won't eat it."

—TRICIA, WHITE PLAINS, NY

"**I LOVE HIM, BUT...**"

66**H**e wipes his mouth on his sleeve. His hands on his pants. If I complain, he laughs and says he's just a 'country boy.' "

—MAUREEN, PHOENIX, AZ

"He's fanatic about vegetables. He spends hours, literally, in the produce market searching for the perfect eggplant, the flawless portobello. He touches, smells, ogles them. If I ask him to run out for a head of lettuce, I probably won't see him for the rest of the day."

—RONA, NEW YORK, NY

66 **H**e puts four teaspoons of sugar in his coffee and he doesn't even stir it. So there's this sticky puddle of sugar at the bottom of the cup."

—NICOLE, TULSA, OK

"He won't eat anything that ever walked, crawled or swam. Nothing that has preservatives, artificial flavoring or coloring will ever cross his lips. Fruits and vegetables must be organically grown. I go along with him—it's a healthy diet. But I crave a dripping, juicy burger. Drowning in ketchup. With a diet Coke."

—KATHY, LOS ANGELES, CA

66He eats off my plate.
I have to gobble my
meal before he swipes it."

—CLAIRE, TOLEDO, OH

66 **W**hatever the kids leave on their plates goes into his mouth. Chunks of fat, crusts of bread, wads of butter. Brussels sprouts. Nothing that can be swallowed gets thrown out."

—MIRIAM, SIOUX CITY, IA

"I don't know why I give him a plate. His food expands off his plate onto the table. Rolls, crumbs, chicken legs, bones are all over his placemat. Even my cat eats more neatly."

—TONI, ALBUQUERQUE, NM

"His idea of dieting is hiding what he eats. If nobody sees him eating sweets, it's okay. I find chocolate bars, donut bags, candy wrappers in the glove compartment, the night-stand, crumpled behind the dresser. I've actually washed candy bars that he's had hidden in his pockets. Not a pretty sight."

—BETH, PHOENIX, AZ

" **H**e eats fast, like it's a race, and belches out loud. When I complain, he tells me I should be flattered—it's a 'compliment to the chef.' "

—TOBY, ATLANTA, GA

66**H**e insists that I scoop ice
cream out so it's level, no
mounds or curves."

—ELISSA, NEW YORK, NY

66 He leaves the kitchen cabinets and drawers open. All the time. If it's dark, I walk into them and nearly get knocked out."

—MEG, ORLANDO, FL

"When he cooks, he uses every pan, pot, bowl and dish. He splatters the counter, the floor and the stove, and leaves the mess for me. 'I cooked,' he says. 'You clean.' "

—MARGE, SAN JOSE, CA

"When my husband offers to help around the house, he asks so many questions and gets so confused that it's easier and quicker to do everything myself. If he were going to boil an egg, for example, he'd ask, 'Which pot should I use?' 'Does it matter which burner?' 'How hot do you set the burner?' 'How long should the water boil?' 'Do you put the egg in before or after the water boils?' 'Do you time it from when you put the egg in or from when the water boils?' 'How much water do you put in?' 'Which egg should I use?' 'Where're the eggs?' 'Where's the pot?' 'How long does it have to boil again?' "

—CYNTHIA, BOCA RATON, FL

"I wonder if he plays stupid so I'll have to do things for him. What takes me one pan to fry takes him eighty-six. Once he made gravy. He splattered the flour and juice all over the kitchen. I had to pry the stuff off the counters with a knife."

—RANDY, NEWTOWN SQUARE, PA

"I LOVE HIM, BUT..."

66 He says, 'Here. Let me show you how to do this.' Whether I'm peeling an orange or scrambling an egg, he has to show me that he has a better way. More efficient. Easier. The most infuriating part is that he's usually right."

—JILL, EVANSTON, IL

66 **H**e never checks the status of the dishwasher. He puts dirty dishes in with clean ones, or unloads dirty dishes onto the shelves, so I end up washing everything all over again."

—MYRTLE, TALLAHASSEE, FL

"He rewashes dishes I've washed, rewipes counters I've cleaned, reorganizes cabinets and cupboards I've filled, rearranges knickknacks on the shelves. Once, I moved the coffeemaker to the other side of the kitchen counter to make more room to cook. The next morning, sure enough, he'd moved it back."

—JUDY, MINNEAPOLIS, MN

"**I LOVE HIM, BUT...**"

66**H**e stares into the refrigerator and tells me we're out of ketchup. He truly doesn't see the ketchup, even though it's right in front of his face. When he finally does see it, he says 'Men are not genetically predisposed to seeing details, as men are hunters and women are gatherers.' "

—BUNNY, CHARLOTTE, NC

66 **W**hen he 'helps,' he inevitably botches the job. Let's say he does the laundry. He *might* remember to sort the colors, but then he'll forget to check the water temperature or level. Or he'll shrink things in the drier. *If* he folds the clothes, he won't sort them in piles, so I have to go through it anyhow. And if I say one *word* to help, he'll snap, 'Okay. From now on, do it yourself. I was just trying to help.' "

—MELANIE, TALLAHASSEE, FL

66 **I**f I ask him to help with something, he ignores me. If I ask him again, he complains that I'm a nag. "

—EVE, BRONX, NY

66 **I** make a list for him to take to the market. It's got three items on it. He'll forget the list. He'll forget what was on the list. But he'll remember to bring home three items, none of them right."

—MARGIE, MINNEAPOLIS, MN

66 **I**f he goes to the grocery store, he brings home bags full of donuts, cookies, chips, candy bars, popcorn. Every kind of junk food. But you won't find a single vegetable. Nothing healthy."

—JANICE, WARREN, OH

"Errands that should take ten minutes take him hours. Later, he'll explain that the prescription wasn't ready yet, so he wandered into a store and looked at some shirts. Then he remembered that we needed a turkey baster, so he went to get one, and then he remembered the prescription so he went back for it, but by then he was hungry, so he stopped for some cold cuts for lunch. In his mind, by bringing me a turkey baster and a half-pound of sliced ham, he *helped* me. Saved *me* all kinds of time. Meantime, I'm stuck waiting for him."

—JODIE, LAKE GENEVA, WI

"He has to fix everything himself. A do-it-yourselfer. But he's also a procrastinator. The lawn's a foot high, only two of our four bathrooms work, and the wood on the deck needs to be treated. When he finally tried to fix a leak in the sink, it took him ten days of failures before he finally let me call a professional. By then the cabinet wood had warped and water'd soaked under the tiles."

—MARLENE, GLENVIEW, IL

66 **H**e's big on gadgets. Timers. He sets a timer for the coffeemaker. So every morning, I'm racing against the timer, trying to get done exercising or doing the laundry before the damn thing turns my coffee off. He also sets a timer for the outdoor lights. I can't turn them on or off—the switches are controlled by the timer. You can break a leg trying to make your way down the path at night."

—PENNY, DENVER, CO

66 **H**e's very security minded. We have alarm systems all around the house. Every few months, in the middle of the night, a deer or a raccoon will wander too close. Beacons flash, sirens blare. The neighbors scream at us and we've got the police at our door. But we're 'safe.' "

—TAMMY, GLOUCESTER, MA

"I LOVE HIM, BUT..."

"When I'm on the phone, he paces, looks at his watch, rolls his eyes, looks at his watch again, stands over me breathing and, if I'm still talking, he creates a crisis or cries out in pain to distract me. He may have gotten a mosquito bite, or misplaced his reading glasses. But the commotion works. He gets my attention."

—KAYE, ST. LOUIS, MO

"He participates in my phone calls. He interrupts to add something or make comments. 'You forgot to tell her about such and such' or 'What about so and so?'"

—LILLY, NEW YORK, NY

"He never responds when I talk to him. So I repeat myself, because I don't think he's heard me. Then he tells me I'm repeating myself."

—PAULETTE, GLENVIEW, IL

"He's got 'wife deafness.' I can be sitting right next to him, talking in a normal voice, and he doesn't hear a word I say. But if I go into the kitchen and open a can of Coke, he'll hear it and shout, 'Can you get me some, too?' "

—THELMA, BALTIMORE, MD

66 **H**e complains that he needs his own 'space.' I'm not to lie on his pillow—he's marked it with his name. I'm not to use his comb or tube of toothpaste, or rinse my mouth with his cup. And Lord help me if I ever touch his razor."

—SHEILA, BOCA RATON, FL

"He's afraid of his ex-wife. He acts like an obedient child when she's around. One night, at a party, she'd had a few too many. She grabbed my husband's arm and sighed, 'Time to go, Honey.' I stepped up, retrieved his arm and pointed her toward her new husband, reminding her that she had the wrong guy. If I hadn't, I'm not saying that he'd actually have gone with her. But I wouldn't have been surprised."

—ERICA, ATLANTA, GA

"He's always in the bathroom. It's his 'office.' He has a phone in there, a small TV, a book-rack, newspapers and magazines. He talks to his broker, his secretary, his clients. All he needs is a computer and he'll never come out."

—REGINA, CHEVY CHASE, MD

PRIVY PROBLEMS...

By the Light
of the Half Moon

The bathroom inspires more complaints than any other single room in the house. Husbands, many wives say, do not *see* their own behavior and have no idea what slobs they are. The same dapper gentlemen who excel in the details of their professions or the subtleties of business leave toilet seats up, splash water on the counter, spray toothpaste on the mirror and discard wet towels or dirty clothes on the floor. They are baffled by the concept of replacing toilet paper. They leave toothpaste uncovered, squeeze the tube in the middle and never wash out the sink. They leave the soap in wet dishes until it turns into slime. Or perhaps worse, they are too fastidious, polishing the mirrors, powdering their feet and spraying air freshener every time someone uses the toilet.

Seasoned wives, however, claim that even the most annoying of their husbands' bathroom habits are manageable because they are stable and predictable, never deviating. "You can take them to the bank," one woman says. "Although I doubt they'd accept the deposit."

66 **H**e's bald. But it takes him twenty minutes to arrange his remaining fringe. Everywhere we go, we're late because he spends so much time on his 'hair.' 99

—CARLA, CHICAGO, IL

66 **H**e trims his chest hair, so it's all even and not too curly. And he trims his armpits, so the hair doesn't stick out." 99

—FELICIA, ORLANDO, FL

66 **I** wonder if he even *sees* body hair. Our bathroom is lined with it, but it would *never* occur to him to dust bust it. It's all over the floor after he showers. Loose hairs fly off his body and land all over the room. They cluster in the corners, cling to the sides of the sink with the stubble from his razor, which is clumped together on the enamel with tiny bits of food and globs of hardening toothpaste."

—ANNA, EVANSTON, IL

"He trims his eyebrows and nose hair and leaves the clippings all over the floor, the sink, the tiles. No matter how many times I mention this to him, he never cleans them up. He thinks he does. I've watched him sweep his hand across the tiles, gathering a few hairs, leaving hundreds. Sometimes I think he can't see them. There's no other explanation."

—TINA, MEMPHIS, TN

"After his hair transplant, he had scabs all over his scalp. They must have itched. He picked at them and everywhere I went, all over the house, I'd find these little crusty things. His scabs."

—AUDREY, RENO, NV

"He wears a rug. He lives in fear of the wind blowing. Even when the air conditioning was broken in the car, he wouldn't let me open the windows for fear his hair would blow off. So we sweated and suffered in a sweltering car."

—CYNTHIA, MIAMI, FL

"His personality changed when he got his hair weave. Now he's obsessed with hair products. Every chance he gets, he checks himself in the mirror. And if he can't find a mirror, a TV screen, a glass cabinet or a windowpane will do."

—MEG, PHILADELPHIA, PA

"When we got married, he had a beard. For the next twenty years, he had a beard. Suddenly, the beard's gone. Off. He just shaved one day. Didn't even ask me or warn me. I don't even recognize him. He's got so much face."

—ALICE, ANN ARBOR, MI

66 **H**e thinks he looks great, but I don't like the feel of his mustache. It's annoying and scratchy. Plus I'm sure there are germs in it from his breathing into it all the time. And from food. Or sneezing. Oh, really, I don't like to think about it."

—TERI, WINNETKA, IL

66**H**e's very particular about his appearance. Uses mousse on his hair, blows it dry. Files his nails. Oh, and he examines his teeth every morning. I don't know what he's looking for, but he pulls his lips wide apart and licks his teeth with his tongue. Maybe he's checking for food. He's very methodical about it."

—KAREN, ATLANTA, GA

"He gargles every morning. Usually that's the sound I wake up to. Enough said?"

—CHLOE, NEW YORK, NY

"His Water Pik's growing things. It's like a science project. Or a penicillin farm. I won't clean it for him, either. It's his to clean. Hell, I don't want to touch it—I don't even like to be alone with it."

—EDIE, BRONX, NY

66There are days he decides that he's not going to brush his teeth. If I ask him about this, he says, 'I'm giving them a rest.' "

—RANDY, CHATTANOOGA, TN

"He never rinses the sink. Globules of toothpaste harden on the porcelain. I'm tempted to chisel them off and serve them as after-dinner mints."

—JULIA, OLYMPIA, WA

"**E**very morning, he clears his sinuses in the bathroom. It sounds like a bark. Sometimes he makes noises so loud I think he's been shot."

—RUTH, WILMINGTON, DE

"I LOVE HIM, BUT..."

66**H**e honks. Every morning, I wake up to the sounds of him blowing his nose. It sounds like a gaggle of geese have attacked our bathroom."

—RITA, CHEVY CHASE, MD

"I LOVE HIM, BUT..."

66 **H**e splashes water all over the bathroom. Washing his face requires him to soak not just the sink, but the mirrors, the counter, the toilet seat, the floor, sometimes even the door."

—CHELSEA, STAMFORD, CT

"I LOVE HIM, BUT..."

66 **H**e sings in the shower. Really belts it out. Oh, and he's tone deaf."

—PAULA, KANSAS CITY, MO

93

"He takes long showers. Half an hour. I don't know what takes so long, but I don't want to go in. I'm afraid I'll catch him doing something personal. You know, like polishing his armor.**"**

—LYNNE, WHEELING, WV

66 **H**e sleeps in his shorts, and every morning, when he takes them off to shower, he blows his nose in them and drops them on the bathroom floor. Where they stay, until 'somebody' picks them up."

—HEATHER, CHICAGO, IL

"I LOVE HIM, BUT..."

"Clogged drains are just fine with him."

—NORA, SAN FRANCISCO, CA

"He never drains the tub. Once I got fed up and didn't do it for him. The water sat there, incubating, for three days."

—PENNY, TULSA, OK

"I LOVE HIM, BUT..."

66 He will not use a bath towel. He thinks it's wasteful. 'Who needs to wash all that laundry?' He pats himself dry with a washcloth. This takes some time, because he's a big man. But he's very adamant about this."

—AMELIA, SANTA BARBARA, CA

"I LOVE HIM, BUT..."

"He's obsessed with keeping the bathroom clean. If I as much as leave a watermark on the bathroom tiles, he's upset. Let alone if I hang up pantyhose to dry or let a strand of hair fall into the sink."

—EUNICE, BILLINGS, MT

66 **H**e's an early flusher. So there's always a little something left over to greet me when I come into the room.**99**

—IDA, PHILADELPHIA, PA

"I LOVE HIM, BUT..."

66 I get daily physical descriptions of his bowel movements. He calls me at work to tell me about them. My lack of enthusiasm doesn't affect him. This is his favorite subject."

—MARIA, CHERRY HILL, NJ

66 **H**e won't let me open the bathroom window, no matter how much it needs to be aired out. In winter he says, 'We'll be heating the outside.' In summer it's, 'We'll be air-conditioning the outside.' It gets pretty ripe in there."

—SALLY, BETHESDA, MD

"My husband insists on opening the bathroom windows, no matter what the weather. It can be below zero with gusting wind, or storming rain. No matter. The bathroom window's open. I've had to wipe snow off the floor."

—WENDY, CAMDEN, ME

"He wraps his penis in toilet paper when he's sitting on the toilet. I don't know why. Boredom, maybe. Or maybe he's afraid it'll fall in."

—PEG, WESTPORT, CT

"By day, he's a mild-mannered accountant. But at night, he dresses up in his NRA cap and takes his *Handguns* magazines into the bathroom. Plays country music on the radio. He has a great time."

—JODIE, INDIANAPOLIS, IN

" **I** guess you'd say he's shy. At parties, he goes off in a corner with his drink and I often find him asleep in an easy chair when it's time to leave."

—CELIA, PITTSBURGH, PA

PERSONALITY...

THE WHOLE PACKAGE

Ironically, what wives love most about their husbands in one context often drives them nuts in another. A woman who admires her husband's sensitive intellect complains that he's too thoughtful, not spontaneous or fun-loving enough. A wife who enjoys her husband's wealth and success in business laments that he's a competitive workaholic, unable to relax. Women who rely on their husbands' dependability fault their predictability; those who wonder at their spouses' depth lament the intensity of their moods, and the same wives who praise their husbands' unwavering positive attitudes deride them for being unrelenting optimists.

Whether husbands are macho or meek, suspicious or trusting, loners or party animals, the very traits that make them irresistible to their women at one moment can make them unbearable at another. Qualities that glistened during the haze of the honeymoon often glare in the light of forever after.

"He has no sense of the future. He's spontaneous, lives in the moment. And that's fun. But his concept of the future is dinner tonight. Thinking about tomorrow morning would really be stretching it."

—PATSY, HOUSTON, TX

"He's a dreamer. He thinks up 'million-dollar' contraptions —like tennis racquets that won't give you tennis elbow, resealable beer cans, car engines that run on human energy, voice-activated household appliances."

—CHERYL, KANSAS CITY, KS

"**H**e's charmingly old-fashioned. He opens doors for women, seats us at the table. Wears bow ties. But he has apoplexy if someone lifts his fork before the hostess or wears anything but white on the tennis court. Poor grammar makes him bleed."

—MARIA, STONE HARBOR, NJ

"No matter what happens, he sees the bright side. If someone dies suddenly, he'll say, 'At least he didn't suffer.' If someone dies slowly, he'll say, 'At least he had time to prepare.' When I'm down, he always points out some positive lesson or eventual possible outcome. Every cloud's got a silver lining."

—EDITH, BATON ROUGE, LA

"He's too serious. Every reaction is slowly, carefully thought out. You can't just ask a question and get a straight, simple answer. Even 'How'd you like the movie?' requires that he cogitate and mull. By the time he comes up with an answer, I've lost interest, even forgotten my question.**"**

—SONDRA, ITHACA, NY

"I can never get a straightforward, honest opinion from him. He always plays it safe, avoids committing himself to any point of view. Like a politician. He goes on and on using lots of large words so that, at the end, you think he's answered you but you're not sure what he said."

—LEE, LOS ANGELES, CA

"I LOVE HIM, BUT...."

66 **T**he good news is that he does everything perfectly. The bad news is that it takes him all night to dry a dish so there are no water spots. Washing the car is a lifetime project."

—SERENA, OAKLAND, CA

"He's romantic, claims that we're two halves of the same person. The downside is that he expects me automatically to know his mood or his schedule. Like I should be able to read his mind. Or, I should say, his half of our mind."

—SAMANTHA, TOPEKA, KS

66**H**e's very outgoing and friendly. If I send him out to pick up a pizza, I hope he doesn't run into a friend. Or it'll be breakfast time before he gets back."

—HILLARY, MONTPELIER, VT

"He so polite, he chats with telephone solicitors."

—CAMMY, TAMPA, FL

66He can't relax. He's always cracking his knuckles, twiddling his thumbs, drumming his fingers, bouncing his knees, twisting his rings, wiggling his toes. He's never still, even in his sleep."

—MARTHA, SOUTH BEND, IN

"He never lets me finish a sentence. He cuts me off and answers what he thinks I'm going to say. And half the time he's wrong, so he's talking about something completely irrelevant to what's on my mind. But even more annoying is that half the time he's right."

—RUTH, LARCHMONT, NY

"He can't say no. If someone asks for a favor, he can't refuse. If he gets into a conversation after work, he'll miss dinner. He doesn't want to be abrupt or impolite. He laughs at jokes that aren't funny. And even if he's not interested, he asks follow-up questions. He overbooks our social life, rushes to help or accommodate others and can't understand why I get annoyed—because he's trying so hard to do the right thing."

—DIANE, CHICAGO, IL

"He always tells me what he thinks I want to hear. He'll say that the kids are ready for school when, in fact, they have on neither socks nor shoes, their hair is uncombed, and their faces are crusted with cereal. He'll say that the laundry's been put away. But I find my socks in a pile. He tells me the bills are all paid, but when I try to use the Visa card, it's rejected at the store. It's as if he says, 'Yes, Dear,' no matter what the truth is."

—FLORA, OMAHA, NE

"He's a poor planner. He'll leave us twenty minutes to make six stops. We're always late. Always in a rush."

—SONIA, WASHINGTON, D.C.

"I LOVE HIM, BUT..."

"He calls home to say, 'I'm leaving the office now. I'll be home in twenty minutes.' Half an hour later, he'll call to say he's still at the office. He's leaving now. This can go on all night."

—LENA, BROOKLYN, NY

66 **W**henever we're going somewhere, he sits in the car and 'honks.' The whole neighborhood knows he's waiting for me."

—ROSE, MORTON GROVE, IL

"He growls at the dog, just to make it clear who's boss."

—LOIS, PHOENIX, AZ

"He's early for everything. When we dated, he arrived half an hour ahead of time. I had to make him wait on the porch. Now, if we're going somewhere, he's dressed and ready to leave before I've even had my bath."

—LEILA, SAN JOSE, CA

"I LOVE HIM, BUT..."

"He thinks how you shake someone's hand is a measure of your character. He shakes hands so firmly, I see people wince in pain."

—CARLA, WASHINGTON, D.C.

"When the phone rings, he jumps for it. Pounces on it. He has to answer it on the first ring."

—STACEY, WHITE PLAINS, NY

"He makes lists every morning, telling me what errands to run during the day. Go to the cleaners or the drugstore or the market. His list is always coded. Cl is cleaners. RX is medicine. SM is supermarket. And then he signs the lists. With his initials. As if otherwise, I won't know who wrote it."

—ALISSA, FORT WAYNE, IN

"He's terribly indecisive, can't make his mind up on anything. Not on what movie to go to. Not on which gas station to stop at. Certainly not on which tie to wear. If you think he's finally made his mind up, close your eyes, count to three, and you'll hear him say, 'But on the other hand...' "

—MARY JANE, WHITE RIVER JUNCTION, VT

"He double checks everything I say. He'll ask me, 'Do we need milk?' I'll say no. Then he'll look in the fridge anyhow. Or he'll ask if the dishes in the dishwater are clean or dirty. I'll tell him they're clean, and he'll examine them under a light. If I say it's raining, he'll look out the window to see if I'm right. He asks what I'm cooking for dinner, but he doesn't take my word for it. He looks in the pot."

—APRIL, FLAGSTAFF, AZ

"I LOVE HIM, BUT..."

66**L**ong silences don't bother him. People around him get edgy, but he doesn't help them out by asking a question or making a comment. He doesn't seem to notice how his quiet unsettles them. Or maybe he does."

—HANNAH, DAYTON, OH

"He does magic tricks anytime, anywhere. In line at the food market, waiting at the doctor's office, at the seashore, on the train. Anyplace. He'll pull a quarter out of someone's ear, find a nickel in their nose. It's not as bad as it used to be, though. He used to do impressions."

—LYNDA, PORTSMOUTH, NH

"When I met my husband, he stammered that he only had t-t-trouble t-t-talking when he was with a w-w-woman who at-t-ttracted him s-s-s-sexually. So you can imagine how I feel whenever I overhear him stuttering."

—ALLISON, BALTIMORE, MD

"When he has an audience, he loses himself completely, loves the sound of his own voice. He doesn't see the glazed eyes, the squirms or the yawns."

—CHARLOTTE, NEW YORK, NY

"Sooner or later, in every social interaction, he puts his foot in his mouth. If I see it coming, I try to change the subject or warn him, but he has an unerring capacity for saying the wrong thing. He's discussed legally divorcing in-laws in front of my parents. Hair transplants, face lifts, eating disorders, religion, abortions, extramarital affairs. He has an instinct for finding whatever topic will be the worst in any given social situation and attacking it with relish, at great length."

—BEV, MIAMI, FL

"He asks blunt questions. 'Pregnant, Sue?' 'Dyed your hair, Wanda?' "

—RANDIE, WAUKEGAN, IL

"I LOVE HIM, BUT..."

66**H**e hangs this huge, ugly key ring from his belt. It has about five hundred keys on it. So you know he's important."

—MARYANNE, PUEBLO, CO

"He tries to protect me from everything unpleasant. So he hides bad news. He wants to 'spare' me disappointment and worry. The result is that I'm always worried because I never know what's going on. To find the truth, I have to dig through layers and layers of sweet, protective sugarcoating."

—THELMA, NAPLES, FL

"No joke is too raunchy for him. The grosser, the better."

—PENNY, TULSA, OK

"When he wants to be cool, he pretends to swing a golf club, like Johnny Carson did. Or he dances like Ali, pretending to punch."

—MONA, MILWAUKEE, WI

"He explains punch lines."

—BESS, LOUISVILLE, KY

"He's a practical joker. He just can't help it. He'll put prudish guys on mailing lists for girlie magazines. Or right wingers for liberal causes. He thinks it's a hoot. A guy in his office was climbing too fast, using everybody around him, so my husband and his pals made up letterhead stationery and sent him notification that he'd won a national award for professional achievement from some fake organization. They all congratulated him and made a big deal out of it—and even the guy's secretary believed it and made reservations for him to go to Dallas to accept it."

—ELLEN, CLEVELAND, OH

66**H**e truly believes that there's no such thing as a 'bad' pun."

—ELEANOR, NEW HAVEN, CT

"Everything's subject to humor. Nothing's sacred. At a funeral, he'll put on a somber face and remark, 'Well, Uncle Joe finally escaped the IRS.' Or in the middle of a wedding, he'll comment, 'Everyone in her family looks alike. How can he be sure which one he's marrying?'"

—CAROL, ANN ARBOR, MI

66 **H**e can not tell a joke. He always ruins the punch line. Forgets it, botches it. Or halfway through, he remembers it and breaks up laughing, leaving the other people sitting there, wondering what he's laughing about."

—JESSICA, SELMA, AL

"Fart jokes. He's got a million of them."

—PATSY, KANSAS CITY, MO

"I LOVE HIM, BUT..."

"He wears white socks. Even with a suit. He says his feet can 'breathe' better."

—DANI, GARY, IN

"He's picky about his socks. His jeans can be torn, his sweater moth-eaten, his shirt old and frayed, but no matter what, his socks must be perfect, fresh, clean and silky up to his knees."

—ANNIE, NEW YORK, NY

"He wears wingtips and black socks. Even in hot weather, with shorts. Like a refugee from some accounting firm."

—POLLY, EVANSTON, IL

"He never wears socks. Even in cold weather, I have to argue with him to get him to cover his feet. Even with a suit, he tries to sneak out without socks. We gave a formal party for my parents. He wore a tux, barefoot."

—MOLLY, COVINGTON, KY

"**H**e goes outside wearing only his string bikini underwear. He struts and swaggers around, getting the newspaper or the mail, or just hanging around. He says clothes aren't normal when you live in a warm climate."

—FAITH, BOCA RATON, FL

"I LOVE HIM, BUT..."

"His shoes must be freshly polished or he won't go out. He wants to be able to see his reflection in them. The house stinks of shoe polish and we're late everywhere we go."

—KAREN, ATLANTA, GA

66He's a slob. He couldn't care less about clothes. Being comfortable's all that counts. Threadbare polyester's fine. Checks and plaid, golden. If I complain, I'm a nag.**"**

—JILL, BISMARCK, ND

"**H**e has a thing about his hands. They must be immaculate and perfectly manicured, clear nail polish and all."

—CARLA, BOSTON, MA

"One look at his hands and you know all you need to know. Cuticles are raw and picked, nails bitten to the knuckles. Like, you wouldn't exactly assume that he's a laid-back kinda guy."

—TERI, TALLAHASSEE, FL

"He hates tomatoes. Won't go near them, won't touch them. Won't eat anything that's been on the same plate with them."

—CATHY, PIERRE, SD

"He's a walking first-aid kit. He always carries medicine, band-aids, allergy medicine, headache medicine, vitamins. For emergencies."

—MYRNA, DE KALB, IL

66 **H**e only gives me faux jewelry. Even my engagement ring is a fake. He says you never know what can happen—why tempt somebody to rob you? I guess he figures that if I get shot for my diamonds, at least he'll have the satisfaction of knowing that the real ones are locked up in the safe."

—BOBBETTE, BILOXI, MS

"He thrives on catastrophes—as long as they're someone else's. Lightening struck a building a few blocks away and he was there, all macho, a hero, helping put out the fire. But at home, if there's a strange noise downstairs in the night, he pulls up the blanket and says 'What's that?' and sends me to go see."

—BRENDA, LINCOLNWOOD, IL

"He's useless in a crisis. Last winter a water pipe broke and was flooding. He woke up in the middle of the night. He started kicking the furniture and yelling, 'Why do these things happen to me?' I got up, called the plumber, turned off the water and swabbed the floors while he ranted about fate and bad luck. By the time he pitched in, the work was pretty much done."

—LENA, NEW YORK, NY

"Waste is his middle name. He won't eat a leftover. Or blow his nose in the same tissue twice. He throws the soap out when there's half a bar left, the toothpaste or ketchup bottles when they're still half full."

—KAREN, BROOKLYN, NY

"**H**e thinks he's 'unpredictable.' He believes that he keeps me guessing. Brags that he's his own man, answering to nobody. But from the moment he opens his eyes in the morning, I can tell you what time he'll be home that day, what he'll wear, even what he'll want for dinner. He's an open book."

—GEORGIA, NILES, IL

"He buys me this contraption some madam would wear—I don't even know what you'd call it. It has zippers and slits. He wants me to try it on but I won't. Hell, I'm embarrassed to return it, much less wear the thing."

—MAXINE, CHERRY HILL, NJ

BEDTIME...

PILLOW TALK

In the privacy of the marital bedroom, wives endure snoring, teeth grinding, sleep-talking and moaning. Many spend hours counting sheep while their sleeping spouses sputter, kick, twitch, toss, steal the covers or sprawl possessively across the whole bed. Some insomniac husbands spend nights pacing, eating, rattling papers and book pages, banging drawers, smoking, flipping television channels and turning the water or the lights on and off. Others fall asleep too easily, during conversations, immediately after sex or even *before*. And on the subject of sex, husbands want too much or not enough, are too kinky or too conservative, too passive or controlling, climax too quickly or not quickly enough.

Wives object to morning breath, liquor breath, cigarette or onion breath. They gripe about kisses that are too slurpy, dry, automatic or infrequent. But banal or bizarre, petty or peculiar, most bedroom complaints are accompanied by twinkles of affection, smiles and tolerant shakes of the head.

66**E**very night, settling in, he grunts. I lie there waiting for him to quiet down. He sighs a long sigh and groans the same, predictable words every single night. 'Oh, bed, bed, bed, bed, bed, bed. Oh, bed, bed, bed, bed, bed. Oh, bed, bed, bed, bed, bed. Oh, bed, bed, bed...'"

—ELLEN, CLEVELAND, OH

"He snores. But it's not a simple, even snore. It's much more torturous. There's a loud snort. Then a long drone, followed by puffing. Then silence. I lie there waiting for it to begin again."

—CHLOE, NEW YORK, NY

66 **H**e cuts his toenails in bed and drops the clippings into his night-stand drawer. He's done that as long as I've known him, and we've been married for seventeen years. As you can imagine, the drawer is pretty full, but I'm not going to touch it."

—SOPHIE, ROCHESTER, NY

"He never cuts his toenails until I get stabbed by one in bed. And I have to be bleeding, too. A mere scratch won't do. When he finally cuts them, he does it in bed. Then he brushes the clippings off the sheet onto the floor. Where they stay until 'somebody' vacuums."

—HEATHER, CHICAGO, IL

66**H**e collects his belly button lint. He digs it out as he's getting in bed every night. At first, he kept it in a paper cup. When that got full, he kept it in a plastic bag. By now, he must have fifteen pounds of the stuff."

—ANITA, NAPLES, FL

"He falls asleep on the sofa, watching television. About two a.m., he's nuzzling me, whispering that my nice warm body's turning him into a werewolf. The man can't understand that if he wants to talk about it, he's got to catch me before I close my eyes."

—AMBER, ARDMORE, PA

"In the middle of the night, he'll sit up and nudge me awake, stare at me with great urgency and alarm, and talk to me in frantic gibberish syllables that make no sense at all. Then he'll fall back on the pillow, sound asleep, as if nothing happened. I, however, am wide awake for the rest of the night."

—AMY, AMHERST, MA

"He has a recurrent dream that he's being chased. I know when he gets this dream because he shakes the bed running in place and fighting, punching air in his sleep. When we were first together, I tried to wake him, but he was so deep in his dream that he swung and punched me in the chest. So I don't try to wake him. I wait it out, let it run its course."

—DONNA, PITTSBURGH, PA

"He sets the snooze alarm for six, an hour and ten minutes before he actually has to get up. And then, every ten minutes, as soon as I doze off, we get a traffic report."

—SONIA, WILMINGTON, DE

66 **H**e has to sleep with his feet sticking out the bottom of the bed. He kicks the sheets out, so the blankets go every which way. I can never be just cozy and tucked in."

—AUDREY, LAKE GENEVA, WI

"When he sleeps, he opens his eyes, sits up and talks. He'll get up and walk around, follow suggestions. We've had entire conversations while he's slept. When I was in labor with our youngest baby, he'd driven halfway to the hospital before I realized he was sound asleep."

—SHANNON, HINGHAM, MA

"He comes home from work and whispers in my ear, 'Go put on something sexy.' I'm yelling at three screaming kids, washing sticky fingers, cleaning juice off the floor and sinking elbow-deep in hamburger meat. But he doesn't notice. I'm supposed to slip into a teddy!"

—LISA, PHILADELPHIA, PA

"He wears thong underpants. He thinks this will turn me on. But it's tough to ignore the paunch hanging over the top. Or the hairy behind. Depending on the view."

—MARGE, SAN JOSE, CA

"He insists on boxer shorts. The baggy kind. White. I buy him sexy bikinis or patterned slim shorts, but he only wears white boxers. He looks like my father with skinnier legs. Its kind of sweet, but not a turn-on."

—PAM, TALLAHASSEE, FL

66 **W**hen he wants to have sex, he oh-so-casually locks the bedroom door and starts to lisp. He never lisps at any other time. But when he'th horny, he talkth like Ewmew Fudd."

—RITA, INDIANAPOLIS, IN

"We can't discuss bodies. Can't talk about anything physical. Not gas pains, not orgasms, not cramps, not sweat. Nothing. Sex, bodies, the grisly stuff that life is built from is just something 'one' doesn't mention. So obviously, a lot goes unsaid."

—JUDY, MINNEAPOLIS, MN

"He won't lock the bedroom door. He has to be 'spontaneous.' One Sunday morning, while he was being 'spontaneous,' I heard giggling. Our kids, ages four and three, had been hiding under the bed, waiting to surprise us when we woke up. 'What was all the bouncing?' they wanted to know."

—JILLIAN, RANDOLPH, VT

"He bounces out of bed in the morning, talking, as if we're in the middle of a conversation. He picks up where we left off, maybe the night before, maybe a week before. It never occurs to him that I might still be asleep. To him, he's up and it's party time."

—TOBEY, TOLEDO, OH

"Before we can make love, he must complete his 'toilet.' This ritual is always the same. It never deviates, night after night. It takes twenty-five minutes. So there I am, feeling romantic, waiting, trying to sustain my mood for what I know will be twenty-five minutes. And I hear his Water Pik, the flooshing and splooshing and gurgling of water in his throat. I hear him flossing and by the time he comes in, I'm just not in the mood."

—ROSE, MORTON GROVE, IL

"No matter what we're doing, he won't miss a phone call. He'll never let the answering machine take a call. Even if we're making love! He'll conduct conversations with, say, his mother or his golf buddies, right in the middle."

—KERRIE, NEW ORLEANS, LA

66 **S**ex, to my husband, is a spiritual encounter. Intense. But he sees it as a depletion of the spirit and contamination of the body. So he purifies himself afterward. He goes into the cellar, burns incense and rubs oils on his body, meditates, chants. If not for me, he says, he'd have been a monk."

—KATHY, LOS ANGELES, CA

"I LOVE HIM, BUT..."

"Sex depends on sports. We have our best sex after he's been watching sports with his buddies. Drinking beer all day and hooting and hollering. If the team wins, sex will be great. But if it was a bad game, forget it."

—PATSY, HOUSTON, TX

"He stands in front of the mirror, practicing what he calls his 'sexy look.'"

—SYLVIA, EVANSTON, IL

"He lifts weights. Pumps. Then he poses for himself in the mirror. Flexes in those muscle-man positions. He raves about his 'definition,' his pecs. 'A hundred seventy pounds of blue twisted steel,' he calls himself."

—MYRA, KANSAS CITY, MO

"He used coupons to pay for our anniversary dinner."

—CANDY, NEW YORK, NY

MONEY...

Of Means and Moans

Money gripes aren't really about money; they are about the *meaning* of money. In fact, the role of money as actual currency seems relatively trivial.

For some, money is a sign of power; for others, a measure of independence. Security, success, sexuality, selfishness, competition, ambition— all are written on the faces of dollar bills.

Wives complain of hoarding husbands and splurging spouses, of men who splash cash around or stashed it away, of husbands who use money to manipulate others, elevate themselves, attract attention or secure obscurity. Whether it symbolizes their ideals or illusions, their dreads or their dreams, money speaks volumes. Most wives see it as a mirror that, in a material way, reflects the intangible, unalterable stuff of which their marriages—or at least their husbands—are made.

"I might as well accept him as he is," one wife signs. "Really, the only change he's likely to make is for a five."

66**W**hen I want to talk about finances, he scowls and mutters that money is something to have, not something to discuss."

—JUDY, MINNEAPOLIS, MN

"I LOVE HIM, BUT..."

66 **H**e insists that people judge you by the price of your shoes and your briefcase, so he spends a fortune to 'look' successful."

—ROBIN, CHICAGO, IL

66 **I**f it's not expensive, not a status symbol, he doesn't want it. An empty room is better than one that's furnished modestly. He'd wear a frayed designer shirt, but never a brand-new one off the rack."

—VIRGINIA, BROOKLYN, NY

"He couldn't care less about appearances. Dresses like a bum. Says, 'Who do I have to impress?'"

—JAMIE, LOS ANGELES, CA

66 **H**e spends hours clip-
ping coupons from
the Sunday paper, then uses
them to buy a dozen things we
don't need and brags that he's
'saved' four dollars."

—GAIL, SKOKIE, IL

66 **I**'m afraid to take anything
off a grocery shelf. He cries
out, 'Wait, I have a coupon for
that!' Then he searches until the
ice cream melts and the lettuce
wilts."

—JOHANNA, JENKINTOWN, PA

66 **W**hen he goes for a run, he carries his cash in his socks. Then if I need cash, he hands me a soggy twenty."

—JOAN, ATLANTA, GA

"He refuses to accept that raising a family costs. Living costs. He gripes about the grocery bills. About the price of school supplies, birthday gifts or shoes. And you should see the roof fly when I take the kids to the dentist."

—MAGGIE, TOWSON, MD

"I LOVE HIM, BUT..."

66 **H**e doles out money like it's his lifeblood. The kids have to plead for their allowance."

—MARGE, SEATTLE, WA

"He'll buy anything to save a dime. Day-old bread, the cheapest gas, thin bathroom tissue, meat specials—even if the steak's green."

—LOTTIE, NEW YORK, NY

66**H**e leaves the car two miles away to avoid paying for parking, in rain, sleet, hail or snow."

—CELIA, CHICAGO, IL

66 **H**e hates to pay for parking. We'll be late to a movie rather than park in a lot. If he can't find a free spot, even after driving miles, he'll turn around and come home rather than pay." 99

—BAMBI, SHREVEPORT, LA

"He serves cheap booze out of a Chivas bottle and wants me to buy gifts at discount stores and wrap them in boxes from expensive department stores."

—WENDY, BROOKLINE, MA

"I LOVE HIM, BUT..."

66 **P**arting with money isn't easy for
him. When we have to buy some-
thing, whether it's a tennis racquet, a toast-
er oven or underpants, he'll shop around
for the best price. He's convinced there's
always a better deal."

—ELLEN, CLEVELAND, OH

"I LOVE HIM, BUT..."

66 He'll never say no to a buddy. He lends out money without reservation and never asks to be paid back. It's a matter of 'honor,' he says. 99

—TOBY, ATLANTA, GA

"He tips everybody. Doormen love him."

—ANNA, EVANSTON, IL

66 **W**henever we're out with another couple, he'll say, 'Dinner's on me. Have another drink. I'll get the tip.' He busts the budget and then he's amazed when the credit card bills come in."

—LISA, PHILADELPHIA, PA

"He carries great wads of cash. Pays for a beer with a hundred-dollar bill."

—KATHY, MISSOULA, MT

66 **W**hen his pocket's full, he buys anything. It's as if the money's too heavy and he wants to unload."

—HEDDY, SANTE FE, NM

"I LOVE HIM, BUT..."

"He blows fortunes on gizmos. Gadgets. Thingamajigs. Whoozama-bobs. I don't know what most of the stuff is! I wonder if he does."

—CALLIE, TALLAHASSEE, FL

66 **H**e fritters money away. Buys himself caps, books, magazines. Gets the kids T-shirts, notebooks, markers, candy. Whenever he goes out, he has to buy something. Bagels. Batteries. Shoelaces. He can't come home empty-handed."

—LESLIE, SEATTLE, WA

"He can't hold on to a dime. On a Saturday afternoon, he'll take the kids for a drive. Poof. Twenty, thirty bucks gone, without a thing to show for it."

—SHELLEY, ATLANTA, GA

"When he goes shopping, he takes a list, but he buys extra. If it says 'eggplant,' he'll buy six—and forty-seven other vegetables that I've never even heard of. 'Ice cream,' to him, means at least four flavors. 'Hamburger' inspires him to bring enough to feed a regiment. And twice as many buns."

—LYNDA, CHERRY HILL, NJ

"**O**n Christmas, he spends thousands, literally, on gifts. There's torn gift wrap, wall to wall, up to your shoulders. You have to wade through it. The children get lost in it, buried, stepped on. They dive into the wrapping and like it more than the presents. And then, after it's all over, I have to return everything because it's abominable stuff. Green polka-dot cashmere, mink slippers. Twenty boxes from twenty stores."

—REGINA, COLUMBUS, OH

"He doesn't pay the bills until they threaten to shut off the electricity or repossess the car."

—LEIGH, BOCA RATON, FL

"He won't tell me about money problems. I find out that we're low when a check bounces. Or a shop won't accept my credit card."

—JODIE, WHITE PLAINS, NY

"I LOVE HIM, BUT..."

66**H**e doesn't want to spend money on maintenance. He waits till the car's dead, or the furnace is totally broken down. Then he'll get it looked at."

—ALICE, HOUSTON, TX

"He never pays taxes until the penalty and interest are about as much as the tax."

—DEBBIE, NEWPORT, RI

"I LOVE HIM, BUT..."

"He plays the lottery. That's his retirement plan."

—PATSY, NARBERTH, PA

66"He never picks up a coin that's facedown. Bad luck. But he'll climb through mud for a faceup penny."

—LOUISE, YUMA, AZ

"He does our taxes himself. As March passes, he sinks lower and lower into a funk. By April, he's a complete grump. Sometime around the thirteenth, he disappears into his study and doesn't come out again until he's finished. From the hall, you can hear the whirring of his adding machine, the kicking of furniture and the pronouncing of expletives. He comes out just in time to make it to the post office before midnight on the fifteenth."

—SHELLEY, MADISON, WI

"I LOVE HIM, BUT..."

66**I**f he wins at the track, he beams and giddily hands out fives to everyone around him, especially strangers. 'The more I give away,' he says, 'the more I'll be given.'"

—ROSE, WILMINGTON, DE

"He never says no to a panhandler. He says, 'What goes around comes around.' So believe me, they come around all the time!"

—LYNNE, PHILADELPHIA, PA

"I LOVE HIM, BUT..."

66 **H**e's always got a scheme
going. Some new deal or
business concept or partnership on
the horizon. A big break just around
the corner. Some magical way to make
big bucks fast and easy." 99

—CHERYL, KANSAS CITY, MO

66**T**o him, financial planning means figuring out how much to set aside for the baby-sitter when we have an evening out. Retirement? College? You must be kidding!"

—BARBARA, NASHVILLE, TN

"I LOVE HIM, BUT..."

When I sit down to pay the bills, there's always a check or two missing, and he can't remember what he took it for or how much he wrote it for."

—GINA, SAN DIEGO, CA

"He can never remember what he spent his money on. He walks away before getting his change. He can't be sure if he paid with a five or a fifty."

—HALLIE, BOSTON, MA

"He collects pennies. We have pennies everywhere. Dishes, shoe boxes, bowls, jars full. The banks don't want them unless they're wrapped—it takes them too long to count them. But even if they'd take them, I couldn't lift them all to get them there."

—JULIE, SAN FRANCISCO, CA

"I LOVE HIM, BUT..."

66 He can never remember our PIN number at the bank machine. It's only our anniversary date."

—LISA, SAN JOSE, CA

"I LOVE HIM, BUT..."

"If a neighbor gets a new car, he tells me, 'Forty grand, easy.' When we're invited somewhere, he whispers, 'Six-fifty,' or whatever he thinks the house cost. New sofas, new suits, whatever anybody buys, he prices it, and tells me urgently, as if I need to know it, too."

—SHARON, CHICAGO, IL

"**I LOVE HIM, BUT...**"

66 **H**e calculates the long-term cost of dry cleaning a pair of slacks and compares that to the their original price, to see if the cleaning costs more than the pants."

—KELLY, BERWYN, PA

"He feels the fabric of people's clothes. Suit lapels. Sleeves. Sizes up the quality."

—STEPHANIE, AMARILLO, TX

"I LOVE HIM, BUT..."

66 **H**e wrecks my household budget system. I keep an envelope for each expense— groceries, cleaning, gas, school lunches, and so on. Whenever he needs some cash, he reaches into an envelope and takes some. Drives me mad."

—CYNTHIA, BOCA RATON, FL

"I LOVE HIM, BUT..."

"He balances our checking account every month. To the penny. Until it balances, you can't talk to him. Before I married him, I used to round off the numbers in my checkbook. To avoid all the subtraction. I knew how much I had, roughly. But I don't dare do that now. If I did, he'd have apoplexy. He'd convulse."

—DONNA, PITTSBURGH, PA

"He keeps a ledger and records every expense. Every bottle of aspirin. Every donut. Not a dime is unaccounted for."

—LEILA, SAN JOSE, CA

66 **H**e expects me to account for every dime. I don't know where it goes. Parking lots. Gum. A root beer. Fifty dollars just doesn't go far these days."

—NANCY, CHERRY HILL, NJ

"He saves receipts. Wherever I go, there are these pieces of paper. All over the house."

—ARNELLE, SKOKIE, IL

"He doesn't even open the mail. Bills lie there, sealed. Not looked at, and certainly not paid."

—LENORE, DENVER, CO

"I LOVE HIM, BUT..."

66**H**is wallet bulges, makes him look like he's got a major lump growing on his backside."

—PHOEBE, BROOKLYN, NY

"He carries cash all over his body. A little in every pocket. He doesn't want anyone to know how much he's got on him, or where to find it if they're going to rob him. I can't tell you how many damp singles I've found in the washing machine."

—OLIVIA, LAS VEGAS, NV

"He's forever flirting. Waitresses, his friends' wives, my sister, my mother. Even me, if there's no other woman around."

—SHEILA, BUFFALO GROVE, IL.

AMUSEMENTS...

ARE WE HAVING FUN YET?

The biggest complaint wives have about fun in their marriages is that there isn't enough of it.

Some gripe that their husbands' concept of "fun" is limited to sprawling on the sofa with a remote in one hand and a beer in the other. Others grumble that their husbands' "fun" requires either solitude or the exclusive company of men.

A number try to adapt by trucking alongside their men as they bird watch, wine taste, camp, garden, gamble, golf, scuba dive, fish or spelunk.

Others simply take off on their own. "Over the years," one wife philosophizes, "we've shared a lot. Good times and not so good. Love, affection, dreams, children, meals. All our worldly goods. But hockey's his, all his. During hockey season, I shop."

"Every week, unless we have plans with another couple, he says, 'Where do you want to go?' When I name a place, he says, 'No, I don't want to go there.' Or, 'Not again!'"

—CELIA, WILMINGTON, DE

"I LOVE HIM, BUT..."

66**H**e never buttons the second button of his shirt because an old girlfriend told him it was sexy to let a few chest hairs show."

—MARY BETH, DEERFIELD, IL

"He never lets me talk to a waiter directly. He orders for me, even my drink. He says it's polite; I say it's old-fashioned. It's embarrassing when the waiter in the pancake house asks me what I'd like and my husband jumps to answer."

—AUDREY, GREEN BAY, WI

"I LOVE HIM, BUT..."

"He always has his camera with him. It gives him something to hide behind and still see what's happening. And it gives him a job. Not just a job. It puts him in charge, makes him the director."

—SUE, GRAND RAPIDS, MI

"He's always on the phone. If we go out to dinner, his portable rings a dozen times and he takes the calls, chats with staff or clients while I play with my escargot shells. At the beach, summertimes, he wades into the lake with the phone on his ear."

—ANNA, EVANSTON, IL

"**H**e won't stay in a restaurant if we're seated in view of the kitchen."

—COURTNEY, GRAND RAPIDS, MI

"He calls when he's going to be late, unless he's out with 'the guys.' Then he won't call for fear he'll seem hen-pecked."

—HELEN, LOS ANGELES, CA

"Every holiday, I get the same gift. A new nightgown for Christmas. Panties for everything else. Silk, yes. But how many pairs can I wear?"

—DOTTIE, BOSTON, MA

"Once he knows I like something, I get it on every occasion. It's either Savignon Blanc or something with an amethyst in it."

—RANDY, LANAI CITY, HI

"I LOVE HIM, BUT..."

"He gave me a vacuum cleaner for our anniversary. A waffle iron for my birthday. One Christmas I got an umbrella. Another, a frying pan. Mother's Day, he gave me a cellular phone. He's very practical."

—HARRIETT, SARASOTA, FL

"**H**e gets his secretary or my sister to buy his gifts for me. The other day, my sister called and said, 'Phil told me to pick up a birthday present for you. Let's go! How much should we spend?'"

—KIMBERLY, SAN DIEGO, CA

"He always has a 'short cut.' He goes miles out of the way along winding, narrow roads to avoid traffic lights or possible crowding on the highway. With him at the wheel, a twenty-minute drive can easily last an hour."

—LEIGH, SARASOTA, FL

"He never gets lost. It's always my fault. I've read the map wrong. Or written down the wrong directions. Or distracted him when he was supposed to make a turn."

—LYNDA, CHERRY HILL, NJ

66 **H**e never asks directions, no matter how lost we are. He'd rather miss the party."

—HELENE, ST. LOUIS, MO

66**I**f we go away, even for a week-
end, he forgets to pack his
underwear, but he's brought a suitcase
full of work."

—MAURA, MACON, GA

"I LOVE HIM, BUT..."

"No matter where we travel, he searches for the most awful possible souvenir and buys it. Our den's full of coconut-head carvings, a coconut-shell brassiere, lobster-claw salt-and-pepper shakers, a black velvet bull-fighter painting, a seashell-covered tissue box. Oh, and a cigar-smoking stuffed alligator that opens up into an ashtray. A frog-faced fan. A glow-in-the-dark Statue of Liberty."

—ELLEN, CLEVELAND, OH

66 **H**e reads—no—he studies
the junk mail.”

—JODIE, WHITE PLAINS, NY

"**H**e watches cartoons. Saturdays are hour after hour of Looney Tunes."

—SHELLEY, ATLANTA, GA

66 **I**t's hard to get the kids away from the TV when their father's glued to it."

—AMBER, PHILADELPHIA, PA

"He loves the Three Stooges. Laughs out loud. Roars."

—SANDIE, BETHESDA, MD

"I LOVE HIM, BUT..."

66 **H**e'll watch anything. Just so there's movement on the screen."

—CASSIE, FRESNO, CA

"He over-analyzes everything. If I ever go to a movie with him, I never ask him what he thinks of it afterward. He never just likes or doesn't like it. He dissects it and analyzes each scene and character until I'm sorry I asked. In fact, I'm sorry I went."

—GINNY, ST. PAUL, MN

"He lies on the sofa with a book on his belly and a blanket over his head. I know he's alive because occasionally he snores."

—NANCY, WILMINGTON, DE

"He holds the TV clicker in his hand, like a ray gun. Zap. Zap. Zap. He can't stop himself. Right at Lucy's punchline, the Ricardos disappear and we're watching basketball. Before I know which teams are playing, William Holden shows up in an old war movie. Just as I'm catching on to the plot, click—it's a sitcom. I go into another room if I really want to watch something. Or I just read."

—PATTY, NARBERTH, PA

"**H**e never talks to me, but he talks to the television. He heckles the news anchors. Answers a report, say, about the economy: 'Good, good! Go ahead and wreck the country!' Then he lectures the TV screen about what the President or Congress *should* be doing."

—BECKY, NEW YORK, NY

"I LOVE HIM, BUT..."

66 **I** can't ever hear a news report because he interrupts to correct the reporter's grammar. 'You're supposed to be speaking English!' he yells. 'Learn the language! You're supposed to be a journalist!'"

—MEREDITH, BUFFALO, NY

"**H**e gets up ten minutes ahead of me because he has to read the paper first. He scrambles to get to it. By the time I get to see it, it's all messed up. The sections are all out of order, folded every which way."

—SALLY, BRIDGEWATER, NJ

"He complains that I spend Sundays doing the crossword. Lately, before I get to the paper, he's filled in the boxes with the alphabet. Or notes in the ACROSS boxes, like 'WHYD ONTYO UHIT THESAC KWIT HYO URH USBAN D.'"

—ALLIE, BROOKLYN, NY

66 **H**e listens to opera with the volume up all the way. When the sopranos sing, I stay away from the windows."

—HANNAH, DAYTON, OH

"He sets the clock radio to rap music. Says it gets him moving in the morning."

—NORA, WAYNE, ME

"**H**e comes home, assumes a prone position and watches music videos until dinner. When we're done eating, he picks up where he left off, flat on his back."

—LIZ, SKOKIE, IL

"He believes himself to be a fine tenor. And so, at any moment—while he's drying dishes, driving or getting dressed—he blesses us by bursting into song."

—LEILA, RICHMOND, VA

"I LOVE HIM, BUT..."

"He plays the dinner table like it's the drums."

—IRIS, SAN DIEGO, CA

" **H**e holds this invisible electric guitar, hunches his shoulders, gyrates, fingers the air and makes these whiny, plucking sounds with his mouth."

—AVA, BUFFALO, NY

66 **H**e has no sense of rhythm. When we dance, he's all over my feet. He gets insulted if I try to show him the beat, tells me that I'm the one doing it wrong. So I have to choose between hurting his feelings and hurting my toes."

—SYLVIA, ANNAPOLIS, MD

"We swim together, but he crowds me. I can't do laps—hell, I can't even move. He circles me, like a shark."

—SALLY, NEW YORK, NY

"I LOVE HIM, BUT..."

66 **W**henever we play tennis together, he's always analyzing my game. Whenever I serve, I get a lecture. He'll stop the game to mimic what I've done 'wrong' and demonstrate how I should have done it. And when I return a hard shot, he shouts, 'Good, Martha! Good!' as if it's totally amazing that I can actually hit the ball."

—MARTHA, MADISON, WI

"I LOVE HIM, BUT..."

"He pumps iron after work. While I'm fixing dinner, I hear him panting and groaning like he's in labor."

—MYRA, KANSAS CITY, MO

"He runs six miles every morning and walks around the house trailing sweat while he cools down. The kids run away screaming. I keep a safe distance and try not to slip in his puddles."

—BEV, MIAMI, FL

"I LOVE HIM, BUT..."

66 **I** never see him in the summer. Summers are softball. Practice, games, team rallies. He shows up again around Labor Day, depending on the play-offs."

—ANNIE, SALEM, MA

"He weighs himself at least three times a day, checks his abdominals in the mirror each time."

—LYNDA, CHERRY HILL, NJ

66 Nothing is fun to him if it's not risky. Sports events are only fun if he's got a bunch of money on the game. Skiing's only fun if the conditions are treacherous. Now he's taking flying lessons."

—GWEN, SHELBY, NC

"I LOVE HIM, BUT..."

"He's always trying something new. In eleven years of marriage, I've gone fly-fishing, skeet-shooting, cross-country skiing, water skiing, parasailing and scuba diving—all so that I could participate in my husband's activities. I've learned, though, that whatever he's into this year will pass by next year. So I'm forgoing the sky-diving classes."

—JULIE, PENNINGTON, NJ

66 **W**hen we watch a game on TV, he becomes 'the announcer.' Talks in this deep voice and gives his own play-by-play of the game."

—EDIE, QUEENS, NY

"He never comes up from the basement. I hear clanking or banging sounds now and then. But I don't have a clue what he does down there."

—RAE, HOBOKEN, NJ

"**H**e's always at the computer, typing messages and 'talking' to strangers all over the country. I'm on my own, a single parent. An E-mail widow."

—TRUDY, CHAMPAIGN, IL

"He reads cookbooks and smacks his lips. Actually moans at the recipes."

—RONA, NEW YORK, NY

"He loves horse art. The house is full of horse paintings. Pictures of the hunt. Bad, good, old, new. You can almost smell hay. Or worse."

—BARBARA, WEST CHESTER, PA

"Nothing's fun.
Everything's serious.
Even Monopoly is fierce.
I won't play with him, not
anything."

—VERA, ATLANTA, GA

66 **M**y husband leaves parties. He just disappears for a while. Goes off to a local bar with one of the guys, maybe a cousin, maybe a friend, to 'get away from the crowd.' When we go somewhere, I don't dare let him out of my sight or I'll be stranded."

—ELLYN, CHICAGO, IL

"**A**fter we go anywhere, he analyzes who said what to whom and why. Facial expressions. Tone of voice. Timing. Body language. Positioning. Seating. Layer upon layer of meaning."

—GINNY, ST. PAUL, MN

"**H**e has these signals. Two fingers between his eyes means he's getting a headache. Two fingers on the back of his head means he wants to leave. Three fingers on the back of his wrist means 'Shh.' Or maybe it's the other way around—I get confused. Two fingers on his chin means listen to the conversation in the direction that his thumb's pointing. A finger tapping his nose means something, wait—mingle? Move on? Get me a tissue? Something."

—GLADYS, LANSING, MI

66 Nothing, and I mean nothing, can interfere with his weekly poker game. When he dies, they'll have to hold his funeral until Friday. They'll deal him in on Thursday night, dead or alive."

—CHERYL, CHERRY HILL, NJ

66 **H**e talks only with men. When we go out, the conversation gets divided by the sexes. There's woman-talk and there's man-talk. The minute I or another woman starts to say something, he turns away and talks to one of the guys. As if we women can only talk about hairstyles and curtain fabrics."

—DEBBIE, SIOUX CITY, IA

"He doesn't mind a wet diaper. But if it's poopy, he hands the kid to me. If I'm not home, he waits for me to come home. And if I'm not expected for a while, he calls a neighbor to come over and help him. Anything but change it himself."

—JACKIE, ORLANDO, FL

CRADLE AND ALL...

After the Stork

On the subject of children, some couples are at odds from the get-go about whether, when or how many to have. Others don't discover their differences until after the fact, when conflicts arise about roles, responsibilities, traditions, religion, authority, discipline, education, role modeling, gender modeling, goals and values. And although some wives claim that their marriages are enhanced by children, most simply find that children change everything, instantly.

In short, parenting reveals unseen aspects of spouses' characters, provides fertile ground for marital conflict and introduces a new arena for delight, disappointment or distress.

"Kids," one woman remarks, "give our marriage new meaning. Our little guys give us a shared direction, a purpose that goes beyond ourselves. Something more important to think about than what movie to see on Friday night. And much, much more to argue about."

66 He has this need to tell people that we adopted. It's like, 'How do you do? Our kids are adopted.' He goes through the whole story. Fertility tests, artificial insemination, drugs. In vitro. How much it cost. How many times we tried it. Our whole fertility history."

—ILENE, YOUNGSTOWN, OH

66He gives me a really hard time about the diapers. Cloth versus paper. He says we've got a landfill with our name on it just for our daughter's diapers. So I use cloth now, for our son, and he complains that there are diapers soaking everywhere, that the house stinks, or that the diaper service costs too much."

—KAYE, ST. LOUIS, MO

66 **H**e's afraid the diapers will leak, so he fastens them too tight. Whenever he diapers her, I have to redo it."

—JAN, CAMDEN, ME

"**H**e has selective deafness. We have three kids. At night they can cough, cry, sleepwalk, scream, throw up, fall out of bed, even climb over him into our bed. But he doesn't hear a thing. Doesn't open an eye."

—THERESA, WHITE PLAINS, NY

"I LOVE HIM, BUT..."

66 **H**e can't step back and see humor in the situation when the fourth bowl of breakfast cereal hits the floor. Or even the fifth."

—AUDREY, WILMINGTON, DE

"I LOVE HIM, BUT...."

66**H**e can't understand that our son's not him. He expects him to intuit algebra. To prefer Bach. To enjoy gardening."

—HANNAH, DAYTON, OH

"I LOVE HIM, BUT..."

66**H**e compares himself to the kids all the time. 'When I was a kid,' he says, 'there were no pocket calculators. You had to memorize the multiplication tables. We didn't have video games—we played ball.' Like they care."

—MARIA, STONE HARBOR, NJ

"He belches out loud. The kids giggle and imitate him. You can hear them out in the yard."

—EVELYN, LOS ANGELES, CA

66 **Y**ou can tell what mood he's in by the name he calls our son. If he's happy, our son's 'Big Guy,' 'Buddy' or 'Ranger Robby.' If he's not, he's 'Robert' or 'Young Man.' "

—ALEXIS, PEORIA, IL

"Our first baby's due in about three months. Robert wants us to give all our kids Welsh names. You know. Llewellyn, Gwyndyllyn, Gwynnyth. Gwynnevere."

—BRANDY, BALA CYNWYD, PA

"I LOVE HIM, BUT..."

66 **I**f he gives me a break and 'watches' the kids, it's chaos. They can be screaming, pulling out each other's hair, waging food fights, ransacking their drawers. He's oblivious, doesn't even look up from his TV show."

—GEORGIA, NILES, IL

"He naps when he's in charge. When he wakes up, he has no idea where the kids are. Once they locked themselves in the closet and stayed there for hours, until I came home. He didn't hear a thing."

—LIZ, SKOKIE, IL

"He'll fold the laundry in neat piles and put it all away. Randomly. He never looks at the sizes. So I have to go through all the kids' drawers, sorting the T-shirts and searching for their socks."

—ANDREA, SIOUX CITY, IA

"When he takes them on errands, he always buys them treats. I take them with me every day, and I'm not going to buy them treats every time we leave the house. So I hear, 'Buy us a treat, Mommy! Daddy does!' I don't, and they tell me that I'm 'mean.' But Daddy's a great guy."

—JOAN, CHICAGO, IL

"I LOVE HIM, BUT..."

"If I tell our son to go to bed, he says, 'Let him finish his TV show.' If I tell our daughter to brush her hair, he says, 'She looks fine.' The only time I get my way is if I tell them to do the opposite of what I want."

—KAREN, ATLANTA, GA

"He has no idea where the kids are, who their doctors, dentists or teachers are, what they do or eat or wear or who they play with. He knows their names."

—BONNIE, FRESNO, CA

"I LOVE HIM, BUT..."

"You can tell if he's dressed them. Their socks don't match. Their colors clash. Their shirts aren't buttoned right. They look like they grabbed random clothes in a hurry and fled."

—DOLLY, NEW YORK, NY

"**H**e gets distracted and forgets what he's supposed to do. He drives off leaving the baby's diaper bag on the roof of the car, or her stroller on the sidewalk. He forgets what time to pick the girls up after a party or after dance class. He's half an hour early, half an hour late. Never on time."

—MARIA, MYSTIC, CT

"**O**ur daughter's his 'Dollbaby.' She can do no wrong. But the boys get grounded for breathing."

—AMANDA, NARBERTH, PA

"He's a zombie until he's had his coffee and read his paper. The kids don't even talk to him. They act like he isn't even there. Well, actually, he isn't."

—BRIDGETTE, WASHINGTON, DC

"I LOVE HIM, BUT..."

66 **I**f I've been up with the baby all night, he'll tell me to sleep in. But I can't. Because he'll send the twins off to preschool without brushing their hair or their teeth, in clothes that don't fit or match, without their lunch boxes. Once I got up just in time to see him putting them in the car without their shoes. He scowled at me and said, 'I told you to rest this morning.'"

—JOYCE, YAZOO CITY, MS

"I LOVE HIM, BUT..."

66**H**e videotapes every moment of their lives. I doubt if they've ever seen his face. It's always behind his camera."

—JEAN, PHOENIX, AZ

"If I tell our daughter to come in by midnight, he'll tell her she can stay out till one or two but he won't tell me. Then I'll sit up in bed worrying when she doesn't come in at twelve. He's asleep on the sofa, doesn't wake up at two to see if she's come home, doesn't wake up when she rolls in and we argue about her staying out so late. When he finally wakes up it's morning, and the man has no idea if she got home at all."

—JADE, PHILADELPHIA, PA

"The girls have him wrapped around their pinkies. They bleed him mercilessly, squeeze him dry. And he loves it. Thinks that girl should be able to con the shirt off their daddies. He says that trains them to be proper wives."

—CELIA, ATLANTA, GA

66 **E**very summer he takes the kids camping, and every summer he ends up with poison ivy, a hundred mosquito bites, or a sprained or broken limb. This year his back went out while he was pitching the tent. He couldn't get up. The kids had to call a forest ranger to get them out of there."

—LISA, MOUNTAIN HOME, ID

66 He begins complaining about my family months before the holidays. This cousin's too loud, that one's too cheap, my uncle drinks too much, and they're all a bunch of 'moochers.' I'm dreading the day that one of the kids repeats what he's said. Like asking Aunt Harriet, 'Do you really eat more than a regular family of five?'"

—JOYCE, BUFFALO GROVE, IL

"**H**e tells the kids not to expect to get presents on holidays, that he buys them things all year round. He says Hallmark and retailers created holidays. He curses when he gets cards and gifts from them. And at the last minute, he invariably feels guilty and rushes out, buys impulsively whatever's left in the stores. Spends more than he would have if he'd planned. Then he's furious, sputtering, all over again."

—MARGE, SEATTLE, WA

"He gave our fifteen-year-old her own credit card. Now how can that be a good idea?"

—JANE, ST. PAUL, MN

"He claims to be devout and takes the children to church. Then he falls asleep during the sermon. He's been known to snore."

—FELICIA, OAKBROOK, IL

"**H**e tells strangers how smart and talented our son is, how high his grades are, what nice things the teacher says about him. As if people want to hear this."

—LYNDA, STOWE, VT

66 **H**e boasts about how bad the boys are. Makes them sound like six-year-old gangsters. Makes legends out of chipped teeth and broken windows. People laugh, but I can't get a baby-sitter."

—MAGGIE, TOWSON, MD

"I LOVE HIM, BUT..."

66He says a family's a team. We're supposed to support each other, promote each other, and be each other's cheerleaders and booster clubs. So he stands up and hoots whenever it's their turn, whether for softball or a spelling bee. Or hitting a piñata at a party. Whatever. Even at the preschool graduation, while all the other parents were seated calmly, he was on his feet, whistling when they called our daughter's name."

—SUZANNE, CHEYENNE, WY

66**H**is idea of raising kids is putting food on the table and letting them grow. A non-intervention pact."

—CYNTHIA, AMES, IA

66 **H**e doesn't believe in discipline. Children are who they are, he says. They can't go by our rules; they have to survive in their own time, by the rules of their generation. The world, their peers will shape them. We're obsolete. Of course, the kids love this concept."

—MARGE, SAN JOSE, CA

66**D**iscipline's a contest to him. If they obey him, he wins. If he gives in or compromises with the children, he sees himself as losing. And he's a very sore, very sulky loser."

—LYNNE, PHILADELPHIA, PA

"**H**e pays them for helping around the house. I don't get paid for helping around the house."

—HEATHER, CHICAGO, IL

"I LOVE HIM, BUT..."

66 He doesn't set limits for the kids. His father was strict and he doesn't want to be like him. So there's no discipline in our house. When Daddy's home, the kids can stay up as late as they want, watch as much TV, eat whatever they want. Refuse to take a bath. Leave their homework for tomorrow."

—LAUREN, SANTE FE, NM

"He sits and mopes when I nurse the baby."

—BONITA, NEW YORK, NY

"He lets the dog beg, lie on the sofa, eat from his plate, sleep in our bed. We don't have kids yet, but I worry about what kind of father he'll be."

—ANDY, DENVER, CO

"He gives our teenage daughter carte blanche. Permission to go to the mall. Permission to go to the movies at night, even R-rated movies. Permission to take the car. Permission to use the credit cards, the phone. He says it's okay, that she's safe because she's got a portable phone and Triple A."

—PENNY, TULSA, OK

"If he works late and the kids are asleep when he gets home, he wakes them up to spend some 'quality time' with him. He rouses them, giggles and plays, and then it takes me all night to get them back to bed."

—LYNDA, BOSTON, MA

"He encourages their fads. Nine earring holes are fine. Tattooed ankles, neat. Want to pierce your nose? Shave your head? Drink till you're sick? No problem. Want to date godzilla? Great. He thinks young people need to experiment, express themselves, discover their identities. He thinks their energy's 'refreshing.'"

—DARCY, MIAMI, FL

"He's such a kid that he needs even more attention than our own kids. And he gets into trouble more often. He stays out late, won't come to dinner when I call, messes our bedroom, gets the others into mischief. He sulks when he's chastised. I got angry at him the other day for giving them all ice-cream sundaes just before dinner. The seven-year-old said, 'Mom, don't yell at Daddy. He's just a big kid.' "

—CHERYL, KANSAS CITY, MO

"I LOVE HIM, BUT..."

66 If they need help with their homework, he gets right in there and does it for them. Like he has to prove that he can do fourth-grade math. Or that he knows where Antarctica is."

—EDIE, PORTLAND, ME

"He's never spontaneous, always serious. Even a walk in the woods is a serious endeavor. You need gear. You need a canteen, a coat, a camera, a first-aid kit, matches, a compass. He worries about bears. Warns of rabid raccoons. Ticks. Poison ivy. The kids tease him about being so serious. They scowl and march behind him, like little robots or soldiers, and they salute him like he's their drill sergeant."

—ALLISON, BALTIMORE, MD

"I LOVE HIM, BUT..."

"It's always a party. At six a.m., he bounds out of bed, juggles eggs, whips OJ, makes pancakes shaped like Mickey Mouse or the alphabet. He sings, he dances. He leads the kids in jumping jacks. I roll over, hoping he'll close the door behind him."

—LUCY, WEST HEMPSTEAD, NY

66 He wants the boys to think he's 'cool.' He walks like they do. Says, 'Hey, Dude! What's comin' down?' Listens to their music. And he never disciplines them. The most he'll say is, 'Chill.' Or 'Hey, be cool, wudja?' If he wants our son to drive carefully, he says, 'Hey, Man. Your Mom worries. Don't be that way to her. Hear what I'm saying?'"

—NANCY, CHERRY HILL, NJ

"I LOVE HIM, BUT..."

"When he gets home, he wants affection. You know, romance? He comes in the kitchen and fondles me. Dinner's burning. And what am I supposed to do? Stuff the kids into the cupboard?"

—DOTTIE, SELMA, AL

66 **F**or him, there has to
be a definite winner
and loser. He's got to be right
and I've got to be wrong."

—PAM, INDIANAPOLIS, IN

WAR AND PEACE...

ALL'S FAIR

Every honeymoon has an ending. Even in the best of marriages, spouses inevitably have spats. Successful wives say they learned early how to take strife in stride; many, in fact, insist that the freedom to argue is essential in maintaining a stable marriage.

Most fights focus on minor but recurring issues. Skirmishes grow into battles, battles into wars—over how high to set the thermostat, how loud to make the television, who holds the remote, what time to set the clock radio, who showers first, which way the toilet paper faces, and of course, the position in which the toilet seat is left.

Over time, the *process* of fighting often becomes more important than the *content* of the fights. "We never *solve* anything by fighting," one wife says. "We just sort of let off steam."

Whatever they argue about, when the smoke clears and the air cools, most wives feel better for having boiled over. Whether or not issues are resolved, they're able to blow up, make up and move on. No harm done.

"He snarls at me and growls like a mad dog. It vibrates, low in his throat, 'Grrrrr.'"

—LOIS, SAN FRANCISCO, CA

"I can tell in the morning, just by look-ing at him, how our day's going to go. Sometimes he's yummy, sort of like Tom Cruise. Others he's more Robin Williams, you know, Mork from Ork. When Freddy Krueger's on the pillow next to me, I know it's not going to be a good day."

—SAM, OLYMPIA, WA

"He's never wrong. About anything. And nothing is ever his fault. He's blameless. That settled, fighting's easy. I just have to apologize and we can move on."

—DONNA, PITTSBURGH, PA

"**A**fter seventeen years of marriage, even though he knows this bugs me, he will still stroll in an hour or two late, without calling. 'What's wrong?' he'll ask. He feigns complete innocence. As if he had no idea that I wanted him to call. He knows damn well what's burning me, but he turns everything around, so he's the victim of an irrational, angry wife. *I'm* the problem."

—JESSICA, ODESSA, TX

66 The slate is permanently clean. There's no context, no history, no pattern. If I blow up because, say, he left his wet towel on the bed again, after I've asked him not to eighty-four thousand times, he'll wonder why I'm so mad over such a 'little' incident. He has no overview. To him, today's wet towel has nothing to do with yesterday's, and certainly not with the one from the day before yesterday."

—MONICA, LOS ANGELES, CA

"Everything is always somebody else's fault. Never his. And if he's mad at me, it's never just at me. He blames my whole family, my lineage, my ancestors. Especially my mother."

—BETSY, BUFFALO, NY

66 **W**hen we fight, he attacks everything and everybody remotely related to me. My parents. The medical profession because I'm a nurse. The entire state of Florida, where I grew up. All Southerners. All blondes. All women. Hell, all earthlings. Minus, of course, himself."

—TRIXIE, WASHINGTON, DC

" **H**e finds a way to blame my mother for whatever's wrong. If I'm mad at him, it must be because of the attitudes I got from my mother. And if he's done something wrong—however unlikely that may be—we've driven him to it, my mother and me. He thinks any sane man would go berserk, sooner or later, in our company."

—TRUDY, ST. PAUL, MN

"When I'm angry about something, he just agrees with me. He says, 'Yes, Dear...Yes, Dear.' When I tell him to stop, he says, 'Yes, Dear.'"

—MARNIE, SEATTLE, WA

"**H**e laughs at me when I'm mad. Tells me I'm cute. That I've turned red. That I'm going to start a fire."

—SUSIE, RICHMOND, VA

66 **N**o matter what's bothering me,
if I'm mad, he says, 'Oh, no.
Is it that time of the month again?' "

—BARBARA, LARAMIE, WY

"He mimics me when I'm angry. Mocks me. The thing that's most annoying is that he's good, he's funny, and he makes me laugh. Infuriating."

—MARLA, NEW YORK, NY

"Before we can argue about anything, he has to do a certain amount of chest-beating, like a male ape. He yells, hisses, flails his arms, pounds furniture, slams doors, stomps in and out of the room. It's real primitive, but there doesn't seem to be any way around it. No matter how gently I bring a problem up 'for discussion,' he tries to scare the subject away. When he realizes it won't be scared off, he finally settles down and we talk. But first, I have to deal with the 'beast.'"

—DEIRDRE, GLADWYNE, PA

"He thinks he has to 'fix' every problem. If he can't, he doesn't want to hear about it."

—LORRAINE, PEORIA, IL

"I LOVE HIM, BUT..."

66 **W**hen I'm angry, he retreats. Takes a nap. Gets under the covers, closes his eyes and hopes it will all go away."

—CATHY, DETROIT, MI

"I LOVE HIM, BUT..."

66 **H**e can't stand conflict. So he dodges. It's always the wrong time. The kids are there. Or he's in a hurry, has to get to work. Or it's too late, he's bushed. Or he's eating. No matter when I approach him, it's not 'the time' to confront a problem. If I insist, he'll rave about my poor timing, not about the problem itself."

—MARY BETH, DEERFIELD, IL

"I LOVE HIM, BUT..."

66 **H**e wants to make sure we under-stand each other, especially when we're upset. So he gives me feedback. During arguments, he repeats or paraphrases what I say. He sounds like a parrot. I'll say, 'I'm furious.' 'You're furious?' 'You're making me crazy.' 'I'm making you crazy?' 'Stop it!' 'Stop it?' "

—MARISSA, CHICAGO, IL

"When we fight, he brings up everything I've ever done wrong, lists it all, embellishing where he can. And then he blames me for whatever he's done, as if his wrongdoings were merely reactions to me. Even his anger's my fault. Everything's my fault. And then, afterward, he claims that he hasn't said any of what he's just said. If I answer him or begin to defend myself, he seems to have no clue as to what I'm talking about. If I repeat his comments, he looks at me like I'm delusional and denies his own words."

—LISA, BOULDER, CO

"He never brings up a problem. He never initiates a discussion by telling me something's annoying him. But if I'm annoyed about something, he lets loose a torrent of dusty old, pent-up, long-forgotten issues. My problem gets lost in the onslaught. It's as if he's saying, 'I've put up with all this without even complaining —how dare you moan about that?' "

—VIRGINIA, SEWARD, AK

"He's a lawyer, so fighting with him is like being interrogated by opposing counsel. He uses innuendo and leading questions, false assumptions galore. As if there's some invisible jury who's going to congratulate him and say, 'You win!' "

—AMBER, JOLIET, IL

66 He doesn't fight. He just doesn't cooperate. Gets passively aggressive. Doesn't tell me when he'll be home, doesn't clear his plate off the table, doesn't bring in the newspaper. Pours orange juice for everyone but me. And oh, yeah. He doesn't give me phone messages."

—FRAN, DES MOINES, IA

"I LOVE HIM, BUT..."

"He never hears what he says. He only hears my reactions, as if I just decide to be mad, as if I just all of a sudden attack him for no reason. He never notices that he's yelling, never hears his tone of voice or accusations. He simply doesn't perceive his own part of an argument, as if he's deaf to his own voice and blind to his own behavior."

—JASMINE, DETROIT, MI

66 He's a shrink, so it's maddening to fight with him. He twists my words and changes my meaning ever so slightly. 'What I hear you saying is...' he'll say. But his intonation is condescending and exaggerated, or the context he puts my words into is wrong, so I sound paranoid, selfish or bizarre. I wish he'd yell and have a damn fight."

—FREDA, NEW YORK, NY

"I LOVE HIM, BUT..."

"He plays semantic games when we fight. He'll ask a question with a double negative, like, 'Is it not true that you...whatever?' And if I say no, he says, 'Aha! No, it is not not true, means it is true! You admit it!' He loves to tangle words, twist thoughts, anything rather than deal with the problem at hand."

—BROOKE, HONOLULU, HI

"He completely distorts what I say. If I'm upset, say, because he missed a Little League game, he might respond, 'So I'm a bad father, huh? Irresponsible. A liar, completely unreliable.' Then I have to go off on a tangent about how I never called him a liar or any of those things. My original issue, the one that was bothering me, gets dropped and forgotten so that I can soothe his feelings. I suspect that this is his deliberate strategy, but he seems truly indignant, sincerely wounded, and so it works."

—RENE, MACHIAS, ME

66 **H**e gets hung up over the most minuscule details. If I say we're an hour late, he'll argue that no we're not, we're only fifty-six minutes late. If I tell the doctor the baby's got a red rash, he'll interrupt to argue that it's actually pink."

—JUDY, MINNEAPOLIS, MN

66 **I**f I'm annoyed, he says I must have a chemical imbalance like manic depression. Or I must be suffering from hormonal changes, or PMS. Tells me to call a doctor, see a shrink. He'll never just accept that I'm rightfully, rationally, reasonably annoyed."

—ANDY, FRESNO, CA

66 **H**e fights like a baby. He'll shout, 'So's your mother!' He'll insult me, call me names. And he's not above making faces at me behind my back."

—PAULA, SKOKIE, IL

"I LOVE HIM, BUT..."

66 He belittles whatever's upsetting me. He tells me, 'You don't have problems. You don't even know what problems are. You have your health, your kids, a house people would kill for.' Unless they're life-threatening, according to him, my concerns are not significant."

—BRENDA, WASHINGTON, DC

"If he's angry, he's angry a hundred percent. He won't rally for anyone. Not for our hosts if we're out, not for our guests if we're home. I've had to cancel plans for dinner, theater—even trips. He's stubborn. When he's steamed, you can't budge him. You have to wait it out.**"**

—CANDY, PHOENIX, AZ

"**H**e's a lawyer. I hope he argues better in court than he does with me. He can't stick to the facts. He's illogical. He changes the subject, or attacks me instead of the issue. He brings up irrelevant topics, lists everything I've ever done wrong in the duration of our acquaintance. He sputters. He gesticulates. He paces. But he almost never addresses the issue. It's amazing that he has a clientele."

—JOANNE, CHICAGO, IL

66 **I**f we disagree and it turns out that he was
right, he can't let it drop. He's got to refer
back to it, for days. Sometimes, for years. He's
still gloating that he wasn't really lost driving to
our motel in Key West—what, ten or eleven years
ago. He's got to rub it in."

—LISA, HONOLULU, HI

"**H**e shuts me out. Reads a book, turns on loud music, watches TV, plays with the computer. If I talk to him, he raises an eyebrow and glares at me as if I'm a naughty, interrupting child. Eventually, he gets over it, especially if I ignore him."

—SONDRA, PITTSBURGH, PA

66 **I**f we fight, he gets a migraine or diarrhea. Something so I'll feel guilty or mother him for a day or two afterwards."

—ELAINE, WAUWATOSA, WI

"I LOVE HIM, BUT..."

66 **I**f I'm mad, he pouts. Acts like a mistreated, rejected baby. And I'm his mean, mean mom."

—JAN, MORTON GROVE, IL

66 If there are other people around, he emotes and raises his voice. He performs to get sympathy, exaggerates, makes me out to be unreasonable, absurd. He tries to make our fights into a comedy sketch, where he's the straight man, I'm the clown.**"**

—CAROL, ANN ARBOR, MI

"He never apologizes. After a fight, he makes 'nice.' Whatever I start to do, he jumps in and grabs it away from me. The dishes, the laundry, whatever. He keeps this up until he's satisfied that I can't possibly be mad at him anymore."

—DEBBIE, ST. PAUL, MN

66 **N**othing's ever just over. He mopes and sulks for days. If he talks to me at all, he whimpers like a wounded puppy."

—IDA, NEW YORK, NY

66 There's nothing so sweet as my husband apologizing after we fight. There's nothing so endearing as his testing my good graces, or as satisfying as his make-up kiss."

—GRACE, NASHVILLE, TN